HOW TO ENDURE INJUSTICE

Metropolitan Youssef

ST MARY & MOSES ABBEY PRESS

How to Endure Injustice
By Metropolitan Youssef

Copyright © 2025 Coptic Orthodox Diocese of the Southern U.S.A.

Designed & Published by:
St. Mary & St. Moses Abbey Press
101 S Vista Dr, Sandia, TX 78383
stmabbeypress.com

Contents

✳

Introduction

There are conflicts, at all times, between couples, between parents and children, between congregation in the church, between people's families and friends. This is because of the lack of endurance. If we know how to endure and if we learn how to endure one another, we will be living in a peaceful community.

Why has the percentage of divorce increased? Because of lack of endurance. Why was the generation fifty years ago different from our generation? Because they learned how to endure. But this generation does not know this virtue of endurance.

We need to endure because we are living in a world that is corrupted by sin. All of us, one day or another, will be exposed to suffering. If we do not learn how to endure, then we cannot put up with the suffering, we will be bitter, we will be angry, we will grumble, we will be complainers. In this world, we will suffer from sickness, from injustice, from unfairness, from financial challenges, from death and loss of loved ones, from persecution as Christians, from oppression. All of us will be exposed to different kinds of suffering. If we do not know how to endure, our lives will be miserable.

Is endurance a positive or negative work?

If endurance were a negative work, it would be accompanied by complaining: "And so, here I am enduring, man! It is a matter of time and it will pass; work will change one day anyways, and I will no longer be working under so-and-so." All of this is a spirit of negativity, which will lead to bitterness within the heart and will lead to annoyance. You will remain distressed and annoyed. For this reason, the Church teaches us positive endurance. So what is positive endurance? If someone compelled you to do one task—compelled you, meaning, forced you—then you would do two tasks. The second task you do by your own free will, so that you may say to the Lord, "I am enduring this with my free will." You could have said "no" or refused. The Lord Jesus Christ said, "And whoever compels you to go one mile, go with him two,"[1] and, "Whoever slaps you on your right cheek, turn the other to him also. If anyone wants to sue you and take away your tunic, let him have your cloak also."[2] The second action is the proof that my endurance is positive. Therefore, if someone asks something from me and pressures me to do it, and I do it and more, this is positive endurance.

---

1 Matthew 5:41.
2 Matthew 5:39–40.

As for negative endurance, whether out of weakness or in avoidance of problems, I would do whatever so-and-so wanted, because they are difficult, or to avoid problems. I should not understand Christian endurance to be that a person pushes themself and endures, while on the inside they are boiling. All this will result in bitterness of soul inwardly. As for positive endurance, it will bestow peace and joy in the heart of a person.

When we endure, we should endure out of strength, not out of weakness. Endurance is a strength, not weakness; not because I cannot defend myself, so let me endure. No, I can defend myself and I can set boundaries, but I choose to endure by my own will because of conscience toward God.

In the story when they arrested the Lord Jesus Christ, Peter told Him, "Should we use the sword?" and he pulled his sword and cut off the ear of one of the servants, Malchus. So the Lord told him, "Do you not know that, if I want, I can ask My Father to send Me twelve myriads of angels to rescue Me; He would do it."[3] So the Lord Jesus Christ endured not out of weakness, but He endured out of strength by His own will and by His authority. He endured, and He obeyed unto death, the death of the cross.[4]

---

3   Cf. Matthew 26:53.

4   See Philippians 2:8.

1

Types of Endurance

Enduring Being in Need

Numerous fights arise in a family: "He does not want to give me my allowance"; "he takes the whole salary, and I do not know what he does with it"; "Why is he giving me a hard time?"

In the parable of the rich man and Lazarus, the only virtue the Scriptures mentioned about Lazarus was his endurance of being in need. The rich man was eating and drinking, wearing the most luxurious clothes; yet Lazarus was sitting in need, desiring to eat the crumbs which fell from the rich man's table. We stand before the story of Lazarus, asking, "How did Lazarus go to heaven?" The Scriptures spoke of no virtues of his, except his endurance of being in need. And this is what made him enter heaven. For this reason, Abraham said to the rich man, "Son, remember that in your lifetime you received your good things, and likewise Lazarus evil things; but now he is comforted and you are tormented."[5]

And many of the Church Fathers and commentators on the Scripture say that Lazarus was a real person. This story is not a parable, but it is a real story. And it is difficult to imagine how Lazarus was just desiring to fill his stomach from the crumbs that fell from the rich man's table. You can see how he also endured illnesses, his body being full of ulcers and sores. And he endured injustice and the harshness of the rich man, who walked in front of him day and night without paying him attention, not even giving him some food. And it is amazing that when the Lord told us the story of Lazarus, he did not mention any other virtue in the life of Lazarus, except this virtue, that he endured poverty, being in need, without grumbling or complaining.

The virtue of endurance does not exist much these days. A person would say, "My rights! No, you have to defend your rights"; "Do not allow anyone to use you"; "Do not allow anyone to laugh at you." Because of these worldly principles, however, many homes are ruined, and the little children are the ones who pay the price. The adults who are divorced are unhappy; or they quarrel all the time, and there is no joy. It is better rather that a person endure joyfully and let the matters pass, and the Lord will reward them as He rewarded Lazarus, granting him eternal life at the end because of his endurance. Otherwise, would a person

---

5   Luke 16:25.

prefer to quarrel, be upset, and cause problems? Where is the cross? Where is "If anyone desires to come after Me, let him deny himself, and take up his cross, and follow Me"?[6]

Enduring the Forsaking of One's Own Will and Opinion

Some of us, if our own will and opinion were not fulfilled, would become angry. We want our will to be done—sometimes with God and many times with others.

When I remember St. Mary, the Mother of God, the one who is preferred above the cherubim and seraphim, and reflect on her life, I can see how she completely denied her will in her life. She never made a decision, or a choice, for her life. When she was a little girl, her parents presented her to the temple. And of course, they did not take her opinion about this. When she turned fourteen, the elders in the temple chose Joseph the carpenter, to take care of her. She did not choose him, nor did she say no. She went with him, and she had actually vowed her virginity to God. And here the Archangel Gabriel appeared to her and told her, "You will conceive and have a Son." Yes, her pregnancy and delivery did not make her lose her virginity. But she experienced something: pregnancy and giving birth that she never expected to experience. And this again was not her choice,

6   Matthew 16:24.

but done in obedience. When the Archangel Gabriel announced the glad tidings to her, she said, "Behold the maidservant of the Lord! Let it be to me according to your word."[7]

And after this when she gave birth to the Lord Jesus Christ, and they did not find a place, the only place in the end was among the animals. Of course she did not choose this, but this was the only option. And she accepted it without complaining or grumbling. And then an angel appeared to Joseph to tell him, "Arise, take the young Child and His mother, flee to Egypt,"[8] which is a very long trip. This period in their life took three and a half years, and she did not choose this either. When they returned from Egypt, and an angel appeared to them and told them, "Do not go to Bethlehem"—where she grew up—"but go to Nazareth." And if you study geography, Galilee is far away from Judea—two different regions. So she went to a completely different region, and so on. Even at the time of the crucifixion, she did not choose with whom she would live. The Lord told her, "Mary, this is your son; John, this is your mother."[9] And she went with John.

How was St. Mary able to so completely forsake her will, and to live her life without making any choices for herself? This is a high level of spirituality: to endure the complete denial of yourself, the

---

7   Luke 1:38.

8   Matthew 2:13.

9   Cf. John 19:26–27.

forsaking of your will, not making any choices for yourself.

Many people fight with each other, each of them wanting their opinion to be followed at home, and so they enter into a struggle for power. The father wants to follow his own opinion, not the mother's, and so he tries to win over one or two of the children with him. The mother, likewise, tries to win over one or two children with her. It makes you feel that you are in a struggle for power: this one wants to follow their own opinion, and that one wants to follow their own opinion—and fights ensue. Where, however, is the forsaking of your own will? Where is the person who says to the Lord, "Thy will be done"?

Submission always makes the person afraid. In the epistle of our teacher Peter, speaking about submission, he gives the example of our mother Sarah, saying, "Wives, likewise, be submissive to your own husbands, that even if some do not obey the word, they, without a word, may be won by the conduct of their wive,"[10] that is to say, even if the husband does not listen to the word of the Lord, he can be won by the wife when she submits with love. He adds, saying, "When they observe your chaste conduct accompanied by fear,"[11] and continues, saying, "For in this manner, in former times, the holy women who trusted in God also adorned themselves, being submissive to their

---

10   1 Peter 3:1.
11   1 Peter 3:2.

own husbands,"[12] meaning that the adornment with which a woman adorns herself is her submission to her husband. And here he gives an example, saying, "As Sarah obeyed Abraham, calling him lord, whose daughters you are if you do good and are not afraid with any terror."[13] What is the story behind the phrase "not afraid with any terror"? The idea of submission always causes fear: "But what if he exploits me? In this way, I will have no opinion in the house." He is saying that you should not be afraid when you submit, because our Lord is the one who will defend you.

Abraham twice asked Sarah to say that she was his sister, knowing well that if she said that she was his sister, Pharaoh or Abimelech might take his wife and marry her. And why was he doing all this? Because he feared for himself. He said, "Because I thought, surely the fear of God is not in this place; and they will kill me on account of my wife."[14] When someone thinks about it, it is not right: he endangered his wife to be taken as a wife for Pharaoh or Abimelech, all this to save his own life. Sarah could have said to him, "What is this you are saying? You want to expose me to danger, because you fear for yourself. Where is love? Where is the sacrifice?" But Sarah, although she had a strong personality and her word was weighty—she once told him, "Marry Hagar," and he said, "Yes, I will do it," and then she said, "Cast out Ishmael," and he replied,

---

12   1 Peter 3:5.

13   1 Peter 3:6.

14   Genesis 20:11.

"Yes, I will do it,"—but Sarah, when it came to these two incidents, submitted to Abraham and listened to his word. Who would defend Sarah? Our Lord Himself. For this reason, St. Peter the Apostle says, "Do not be afraid with any terror"[15] when you submit to your husband, because, as our Lord defended Sarah, He will defend you also. The Lord will not permit any harm to befall you.

So that no one says that I am biased against women, what I said about giving up one's own will is for both; that is, the man ought to give up his own will, and the woman likewise. If we are speaking about Abraham and Sarah, Abraham loved Ishmael. He was his first-born son, the foremost of his power, and he did not want to cast him out. But when Sarah asked him, and God supported Sarah, saying to him, "Whatever Sarah has said to you, listen to her voice,"[16] Abraham did not argue with the Lord. He indeed cast out Ishmael and Hagar, listening the word of the Lord and the word of Sarah. But someone might say, "But the Lord told him to do so. He gave up his will because the Lord told him." Who tells us to be patient with one another—is it not the Lord? Who tells us to forgive one another—is it not the Lord? Should we not listen to the word of the Lord then? Or does the Lord have to appear to me like what He did with Abraham, to tell me, "Be patient with you husband," or "Be patient with your

---

15   Cf. 1 Peter 3:6.

16   Genesis 21:13.

wife." What is "bearing with one another in love"[17] which we pray every day in the Agpeya?

Am I willing to give up my own will, to preserve my home? Am I willing to give up my own opinion, so that we live in peace together? Or do we prefer fights and the struggle for power? Where is endurance, enduring giving up my own will?

There is a beautiful saying in the Paradise of the Fathers: "The one who bears the dead receives wages from men, and the one who bears the living receives wages from God."[18] The one who bears the dead is like the funeral home, whom we pay when they come, carry and bury someone—they receive their wages from men. The one who bears the living receives wages from God. Who of us is ready to bear others?

Enduring Mistreatment and Humiliation

There are some people who have a huge ego, who cannot endure an offensive or insulting word. And so problems ensue at home if one of the sides is mistreated or humiliated. What do you think of the Lord Christ? He endured being called "Mad,"[19] and they said to

---

17   Ephesians 4:2.

18   *Bostan Al-Rohban Al-Mowasah, Al-joz' Al-Thalith* [The Expanded Paradise of the Monks, Vol. 3]. (Egypt: St. Macarius Monastery, 2006), 419. Cf. *The Anonymous Sayings of the Desert Fathers*, J. Wortley, trans. (Cambridge, UK: Cambridge University Press, 2013), N.335.

19   John 10:20.

Him "You have a demon,"[20] and, "He casts out demons by Beelzebub, the ruler of the demons,"[21] and, "Do we not say rightly that You are a Samaritan and have a demon?"[22] And on the cross, they insulted Him, saying, "Let us see if the Lord will save Him,"[23] and when He said, "Eli, Eli, lama sabachthani?" they thought He was calling for Elijah.[24] He suffered numerous insults, but one of the greatest insults Christ endured was the slap when He was standing on trial, and the one who struck Him did not know that he was striking the God of gods and the Lord of lords and the King of kings.[25] And after the trial "some began to spit on Him, and to blindfold Him, and to beat Him, and to say to Him, 'Prophesy!' And the officers struck Him with the palms of their hands."[26] We say, "Your cheeks You have left open to those who smite."[27] All this mistreatment our Lord endured for my sake and yours, so that we may enter heaven—so that He may take my sins in my place, to bears my sins, so that He may give me His righteousness and make me go to heaven with Him.

To what extent am I ready to endure mistreatment? To what degree I can say as the Holy Scripture, "Being reviled, we bless; being persecuted, we endure; being

20 John 7:20.
21 Luke 11:15.
22 John 8:48.
23 See Matthew 27:43.
24 See Matthew 27:46–47.
25 See John 19:22.
26 Mark 14:65.
27 The Divine Liturgy According to St. Gregory – Agios (Holy).

defamed, we entreat,"[28] to what extent am I ready to endure? You see for example, in the parable of the prodigal son, that older son spoke with his father in a disrespectful and insulting manner, and he blamed him, saying, "Lo, these many years I have been serving you; I never transgressed your commandment at any time; and yet you never gave me a young goat, that I might make merry with my friends. But as soon as this son of yours came, who has devoured your livelihood with harlots, you killed the fatted calf for him."[29] Yet the father answered him very kindly, saying to him, "Son, you are always with me, and all that I have is yours."[30] Who of us is ready to endure our children, to endure our husbands and wives, to endure our relatives, friends, co-workers, and so we live in peace together?

If you are insulted, remember how much Christ endured for your sake, and let the word, insult, and mistreatment pass. This is an opportunity for you to forgive. How would you learn to forgive, and to grow in the virtue of forgiveness, if there were no one to insult you? How could you stand and say, "Forgive us our trespasses, as we forgive those who trespass against us"? The Lord will say to you, "How many people have you forgiven? List the names of the people you have forgiven. Think about it." Then you will say, "There is none, Lord. In fact, I have not forgiven anyone." He

---

28   1 Corinthians 4:12–13.

29   Luke 15:29–30.

30   Luke 15:31.

will answer, "Are you lying to Me in your prayer? You say, 'Forgive us our trespasses, as we forgive those who trespass against us,' and you have not forgiven anyone yet. Rather, you return mistreatment for mistreatment, eye for eye, tooth for tooth, and then say, 'Forgive us our trespasses, as we forgive those who trespass against us.'"

Enduring Being Chastened and Disciplined

The Holy Scriptures spoke concerning this type of endurance, saying:

> "For whom the LORD loves He chastens, and scourges every son whom He receives." If you endure chastening, God deals with you as with sons; for what son is there whom a father does not chasten? But if you are without chastening, of which all have become partakers, then you are illegitimate and not sons.[31]

The meaning of "of which all have become partakers" is that if I am walking down the street and see fifteen children fighting and throwing rocks at each other, and one of these children is my son, then who of the fifteen children will I chasten? My son is the one I am concerned with. But if no one of them is my son, then I will look and say, "Those poor kids," and take a side street and walk away. This is what St.

---

31   Hebrews 12:6–8.

Paul the Apostle is saying, "If God does not chasten me, then I am not a son of God; you are illegitimate."

Then he continues with a verse, which I am uncertain whether it applies to our time or not. He says, "Furthermore, we have had human fathers who corrected us, and we paid them respect. Shall we not much more readily be in subjection to the Father of spirits and live?"[32] If our fathers in the flesh chastened us, and we used to fear them, respect them, and give them honor, shall we not much more readily be in subjection to the Father of spirits and live? St. Paul is saying that if we submit to our fathers in the flesh, should we not submit to our spiritual fathers? If St. Paul lived in our time, what would he see? Nowadays, if a father or mother said a word to their son, he would say, "I am leaving the house," and would talk back, word for word. Where is the discipline? Where is the endurance of being disciplined? It no longer exists.

St. Paul continues, saying, "For they indeed for a few days chastened us as seemed best to them, but He for our profit, that we may be partakers of His holiness."[33] This means that the chastening of our fathers in the flesh might not have been a hundred percent right; rather it was "as seemed best to them," that is to the best of their knowledge; but God does so for our profit. The Lord's chastening is completely for my interest, "that we may be partakers of His

---

32 Hebrews 12:9.
33 Hebrews 12:10.

holiness." But, "Now no chastening seems to be joyful for the present, but painful."[34] Certainly when my father is disciplining me, he is not full of joy; he would certainly be upset. "Nevertheless, afterward it yields the peaceable fruit of righteousness to those who have been trained by it."[35] If I accept the chastening, this will build my personality and will make me a good person.

The Book of Proverbs is full of verses that urge us to discipline or chasten. He says, "My son, hear the instruction[36] of your father, and do not forsake the law of your mother; for they will be a graceful ornament on your head, and chains about your neck."[37] There are very many verses that speak about respecting and accepting chastening. But unfortunately, the chastening by parents in the Christian family no longer exists nowadays. He also says:

> Hear, my children, the instruction[38] of a father, and give attention to know understanding; for I give you good doctrine: Do not forsake my law. When I was my father's son, tender and the only one in the sight of my mother, he also taught me, and said to me: "Let your heart retain my words; keep my commands, and live."[39]

---

34 Hebrews 12:11.

35 Ibid.

36 Arabic: chastening or disciplining.

37 Proverbs 1:8–9.

38 Arabic: chastening or disciplining.

39 Proverbs 4:1–4.

Those who submit to their parents' chastening grow up to be successful children in their lives, but those who reject the chastening of their parents are not successful in their lives. Enduring being chastened or disciplined is also one of the virtues that exist in the family.

Now for the parents, they ought to endure their children, during the period of adolescence for example, when their temperament changes, and they try to have their own personality. We may think that they are resisting us or are rebelling against us, but they are neither resisting nor rebelling: it is the period of adolescence when they are building their personality. They are trying to say that they are not shadows of their father or mother, rather they have their independent personality.

Consider how David endured his son Absalom who was not a teenager. This Absalom plotted to kill his father and take over the kingdom. But when war occurred between David and his men and Absalom and his men, David gave a command to the chief of the army, saying, "Deal gently for my sake with the young man Absalom."[40] This is the Absalom who wanted to kill his father and take over the kingdom. And when Absalom died in the war, David the prophet wept for him, saying, "O my son Absalom—my son, my son Absalom—if only I had died in your place! O

---

40   2 Samuel 18:5.

Absalom my son, my son!"[41] Die in his place—this is the son who betrayed him, and assembled an army against him, and wanted to take over the kingdom, and went in to his father's concubines, and made the people rebel against him. David, nevertheless, was patient with his children. Do we possess this virtue, that we be patient and longsuffering with our children?

Consider if the Lord had not been patient and longsuffering with us, how many of us would have perished? See the right-hand thief for example, if the Lord had not been patient with him to the last moment of his life, the thief would have perished. But the Lord was patient with him; therefore, let us be patient with our children, and this endurance will bring our children back.

Take, for example, Abba Isidore. This saint was specialized in difficult cases. A burdensome man comes to become a monk, like Moses the black. This man they hand over to Abba Isidore, because he excelled in the virtue of endurance. He would be patient with such a difficult monk, while everyone else in the monastery wanted to expel him, saying, "He is unfit for monasticism. Expel him." But when he is sent to Abba Isidore, he would be patient with him. And with endurance and longsuffering, he was able to bring such people back to the Lord, making them repent. Endurance, then, is a wonderful virtue.

---

41   2 Samuel 18:33.

Enduring and Defending the Sinner

If my wife, for example, or my child sinned or made a mistake, to what extent would I be ready to endure, and forgive, and pray for such a person in the family?

Consider the children of Israel. The Scripture describes them as "a stiff-necked people."[42] They were a very troublesome people, and they rebelled many times against Moses, and made a gold calf and said, "This is your god, O Israel, that brought you out of the land of Egypt!"[43] The Lord was very angry with the people, and He said to Moses, "Now therefore, let Me alone, that My wrath may burn hot against them and I may consume them. And I will make of you a great nation."[44] But what did Moses say to the Lord? He said to Him, "Turn from Your fierce wrath, and relent from this harm to Your people."[45] And he said to Him, "Yet now, if You will forgive their sin—but if not, I pray, blot me out of Your book which You have written."[46] What endurance!

Contrarily, sometimes you find a wife who wants to throw her husband in jail, and she wants him stay there and not come out, and she wants him to be chastised. She would say, "He deserves it. He did this and that!" Moses did not say to the Lord, "They

---

42   Exodus 32:9.

43   Exodus 32:4.

44   Exodus 32:10.

45   Exodus 32:12.

46   Exodus 32:32.

deserve it. Destroy them, Lord. They ascribed Your glory to the gold calf. I am waiting, Lord; punish them." But Moses said to Him, "Lord, if You are not forgiving them, I am not going to heaven with them. Either we go to heaven together, or blot out my name from the book of life." Who can say such a word?

St. Paul the Apostle said a similar word in Romans: "I have great sorrow and continual grief in my heart. For I could wish that I myself were accursed from Christ for my brethren."[47] What a marvelous endurance!

Enduring Trials

Let us suppose that someone becomes sick. You find that the family begins to be upset with God, and they might say offensive words against God before others. It is like story of Job. When he suffered from sicknesses, his wife did not endure. Yes, I seek to excuse her: she lost her children, and lost her wealth, and her husband was sick, and it seemed that he was not going to get better. If you sit and think about Job's wife, she truly passed through very many trials. I can find excuses for her, but not for her saying to Job, "Curse God and die!"[48]

On the day when everything is going well, and we have plenty, and we have blessings, we accept these from the Lord. If the Lord, however, permits that we

---

47   Romans 9:2–3.

48   Job 2:9.

go through a few trials, then we do not accept, and we rebel. Many a time when a trial comes upon us, we do not endure it. Instead of encouraging each other, and supporting each other, and standing by each other, when a trial comes, we rather complain, and harden each other's heart against the Lord, and harden each other's heart against the Church, our friends, and our neighbors. If a trial comes upon us, for example, from one of our friends or relatives, we all boycott that person and stop speaking with them. How are we Christian and do such a thing? Where is, "bearing with one another in love, endeavoring to keep the unity of the Spirit in the bond of peace"?[49]

Enduring Waiting for the Lord

The Lord might give a promise, but the person seems to have no endurance to wait. For example, the Lord gave a promise to Abraham and Sarah, saying, "I will give you offspring from Sarah."[50] But they did not endure, and so Sarah said to him, "That is enough. We are now advanced in age. Go and marry Hagar, and we will obtain children by her."[51] We, however, pray in one of the psalms of the Twelfth Hour, saying, "My soul waits for the Lord more than those who watch for the morning—yes, more than those who watch for

---

49   Ephesians 4:2–3.

50   See Genesis 15:4–5.

51   See Genesis 16:1–4.

the morning. O Israel, hope in the LORD."[52] And in another psalm, we say, "Wait on the LORD; be of good courage, and He shall strengthen your heart; wait, I say, on the LORD!"[53] This is a virtue that is called the virtue of waiting for the Lord.

In Isaiah, there is a very beautiful verse that says, "He gives power to the weak, and to those who have no might He increases strength."[54] The weak means the sick or weary, and the Lord strengthens the one who has no might. "Even the youths shall faint and be weary, and the young men shall utterly fall, but those who wait on the LORD shall renew their strength; they shall mount up with wings like eagles, they shall run and not be weary, they shall walk and not faint."[55] This is the virtue of enduring waiting on the Lord. Do we wait on the Lord. When we enter into trial, do we wait on the Lord? He said, "Call upon Me in the day of trouble; I will deliver you, and you shall glorify Me."[56]

Many times God allows us to struggle with some things in our lives. In order to protect us from falling into pride or vainglory. And some of us cannot endure this. They want victory—quickly. And they do not endure to struggle with sins. St. Moses, for example, struggled with sins for a long time. Likewise St. Mary of Egypt, she struggled with sin for fourteen years.

---

52   Psalms 130:6–7.

53   Psalms 27:14.

54   Isaiah 40:29.

55   Isaiah 40:30–31.

56   Psalms 50:15.

We used to sing a spiritual song when we were young, which says, "If He takes long, He will answer." Even if in the fourth watch, He will answer, but we have to be patient. For this reason, David the prophet says to Him, "Make haste, O God, to deliver me! Make haste to help me, O LORD!"[57]

Enduring Losing a Loved One

Mary and Martha, when they lost their brother Lazarus, they could not endure it. And they blamed God, the Lord Jesus Christ, saying, "Lord, if You had been here, my brother would not have died."[58] But the person who trusts the will of God will accept this, with confidence and trust in God.

---

57   Psalms 70:1.
58   John 11:21.

2

Examples of Enduring Injustice

Lately people have been complaining of the treatment of others, being a little harsh. And some take various means to deal with this. One, for example, might begin to respond in like manner; another might begin to avoid the person, and so on. Therefore, having spoken about the virtue of enduring in general, we will now address the virtue of enduring injustice. Many of us, when we feel that we are wronged, become troubled and distressed.

In this book, we will not be speaking about those who treat others unjustly; rather, we will speak about endurance. Christianity does not encourage injustice, for the person who acts unjustly will not inherit the kingdom. We will talk about how the wronged person can endure injustice.

Jesus Christ Himself

"For to this you were called, because Christ also suffered for us, leaving us an example, that you should follow His steps."[59]

Christ endured, and as Christ endured, He left us an example. And if we are Christians, meaning, following the steps of Christ, we need to do the same thing; we need to do what Christ did: "'Who committed no sin, nor was deceit found in His mouth'; who, when He was reviled, did not revile in return; when He suffered, He did not threaten, but committed Himself to Him who judges righteously."[60] He committed Himself to Him, that is, to God the Father.

What is the example of Christ? When He was reviled, did He revile back? No, He did not. When He suffered, did He threaten? No, He did not. What did He do? He left the judgment to God. He committed Himself to Him, who judges righteously. Rather, He "Himself bore our sins in His own body on the tree, that we, having died to sins, might live for righteousness—by whose stripes you were healed."[61] He committed no sin, but He carried our sins and He died on the cross. He endured the stripes, that we be healed. St. Peter repeats the same meaning, saying, "For it is better, if it is the will of God, to suffer for doing good than for doing evil."[62]

59   1 Peter 2:21.

60   1 Peter 2:22–23.

61   1 Peter 2:24.

62   1 Peter 3:17.

If it is the will of God, if He allowed this, that is, for us to suffer for doing good than for doing evil, then we will be blessed. "For Christ also suffered once for sins, the just for the unjust, that He might bring us to God, being put to death in the flesh but made alive by the Spirit."[63] When we endure like Christ, He will bless us.

The Virgin St. Mary

Another example of enduring injustice is St. Mary. Joseph the elder treated her unjustly, although he had an excuse: Finding a betrothed virgin pregnant, anyone in Joseph's position would say that she had fallen into sin, for there is no other explanation. But because Joseph "being a just man, and not wanting to make her a public example, was minded to put her away secretly."[64] But let her go where? She does not have parents. Where is she going to live? A young lady, who was about fourteen years old and pregnant, where would she go? How would the Virgin defend herself? The fact is that she was falsely accused of this horrible sin of sexual immorality and adultery. And the one who was accused is the holiest and purest woman in the whole world. And she endured this without complaining or grumbling. There was no way for her to defend herself; rather she endured the injustice, and the Lord defended her.

---

63   1 Peter 3:18.

64   Matthew 1:19.

St. Mary endured many things in her life. She endured being orphaned at a very young age— enduring the loss of her parents, for she was living in the temple without parents. And we know the role of parents in raising children, but as a young child, she did not enjoy this parenthood. Also, since she was an orphan and was presented to the temple, she lived a very poor life.

And she endured poverty. We know how endurance of poverty is not an easy thing. You need something, but you cannot afford it. The food that is provided to you is what you will eat; the clothes that are provided to you are what you will wear. And in spite of her poverty, tradition tells us that she used to share her food with the poor and the needy. This means that, although she was very poor, she lived the life of giving, a charitable life.

Also, she endured this very difficult trip from Israel to Egypt. At the time, this trip was difficult, as they were walking most of the time—no shelter, no food. They might have used the gold that was presented by the wise men to cover their expenses on this trip. And they travelled all the way from Israel, through Sinai to Cairo, and all the way to Assiut. And this trip took almost three years and a half. And it was not an easy trip. Tradition tells us that many robbers attacked them during this trip. But she endured all of this.

She also endured the attacks on her Son. I am sure any parent can endure attacks on themselves, but when their children are attacked, the parents are exceedingly hurt. They said about Him that the head of the demons is with Him, and they said that He is out of His mind several times. They wanted to stone Him, to kill Him. She endured at the end the crucifixion. She saw the suffering of her Son on the cross. As we pray in the litanies of the Ninth Hour, "When the mother saw the Lamb and shepherd, the Savior of the world, hung on the cross, she said while weeping, 'The world rejoices in receiving salvation, while my heart burns as I look at Your crucifixion, which You are enduring for the sake of all my Son and my God.'"

And until now, after her departure and after the assumption of her body to heaven, St. Mary endures the doubts people sow concerning her perpetual virginity. She endures when people say that she is not different than any one of us, and that she was born without Original Sin. She endures when people exalt her and make her like God, a Co-Redeemer. She endures when people deny her intercessions, and deny her apparition in Zeitoun, for example. She endures all these attacks against her until now, and in spite of all this, she is called the trusted advocate for all mankind, as we say about her in our prayers.

Also, she endured glory. Enduring humiliation is much easier than enduring glory, because people, once they are exalted or glorified, become prideful. But St. Mary never became prideful, rather she was very humble. When somebody, for example, assumes a high position in the government, separates himself from all of us and treats us as if he is higher than all of us. It is very rare for people, when they obtain a high position or high status, to remain humble. But St. Mary was very humble.

And the glory she received was that she became the Mother of God. Think about this title: the Mother of God. This title, however, did not change her at all. When she went to Elizabeth—Elizabeth was above eighty years old and St. Mary fourteen years old—Elizabeth was like a grandmother for her, and she said to St. Mary:

> Blessed are you among women, and blessed is the fruit of your womb! But why is this granted to me, that the mother of my Lord should come to me? For indeed, as soon as the voice of your greeting sounded in my ears, the babe leaped in my womb for joy. Blessed is she who believed, for there will be a fulfillment of those things which were told her from the Lord.[65]

Can you imagine in our time if an old lady said these words to a teenager? Teenagers are more frequently arrogant and prideful. They think they know better than anyone else. But St. Mary, when she heard these words from this old lady, how did she respond? She responded by glorifying God: "My soul magnifies the Lord, and my spirit has rejoiced in God my Savior. For He has regarded the lowly state of His

---

65   Luke 1:42–45.

maidservant."[66] She called herself His maidservant, although she is the Mother of God. Elizabeth told her, "You are the mother of my Lord," but St. Mary responded by saying, "I am His maidservant." Saint Mary endured exceedingly much in her life. We need to learn this virtue from her life.

Joseph the Righteous

Many of us refuse to endure injustice. Imagine a family consisting of a father, mother, and twelve children. One of these children begins to see visions and to relate them to his brothers: "Look, I have dreamed another dream. And this time, the sun, the moon, and the eleven stars bowed down to me."[67] His father would say to him, "What are you saying? Will I, your father come, with your mother, and brothers, and bow down to you?" Perhaps all of us know the story of Joseph. His father loved Joseph, because Joseph was the son of Rachel who was Jacob's beloved wife. And so his brothers began to envy him and treat him unjustly.

Although they were one family, they began to treat him unjustly. They threw him into a well, desiring to get rid of him. When the older brother wanted to rescue him, so that he does not die in the well, they sold him as a slave to the Egyptians. And they lied to their father, saying, "Some wild beast has devoured him."[68] And then

---

66   Luke 1:46–48.

67   Genesis 37:9.

68   Genesis 37:20.

in Potiphar's house he was treated unjustly again and was thrown into prison, although he was innocent. And he endured the imprisonment. And when the butler and baker of Pharaoh had dreams in prison, he interpreted their dreams for them. When the butler of Pharaoh was restored, he forgot Joseph. And he endured all this. Afterward the Lord saved him, and he became the second man in the land of Egypt. When his brothers came to him during the famine, he had the opportunity and means to take vengeance, but Joseph said, "But as for you, you meant evil against me; but God meant it for good."[69]

Who of us is ready to endure if we are treated unjustly? The Lord will transform the evil to good, as He did with Joseph. He said to his brothers, "You are not the ones who sent me to the land of Egypt, for God sent me before you to preserve life."[70] He had surrendered his life into the hand of the Lord.

David the Prophet

Also another biblical story of enduring injustice is that of David the prophet. It is also a family-related story, because David had married Saul's daughter. Therefore, Saul was his father-in-law, but Saul persecuted David and wanted to kill him. Once he sent people to kill him in his house, but his wife Michal, because she loved him, helped him escape.[71] As the days went by, the

---

69   Genesis 50:20.

70   Cf. Genesis 45:5.

71   See 1 Samuel 19:11–15.

situations were reversed, and the Lord delivered Saul into David's hand. Saul went into a cave, and David was hiding in this cave. They said to him, "It is your opportunity. The Lord sent him to you. Go and kill him." But David said, ""The LORD forbid that I should do this thing to my master, the LORD's anointed, to stretch out my hand against him."[72] And to prove to Saul that he is innocent, he cut a piece of Saul's robe. And the day after, David called to Saul, saying, "My lord the king!"[73] Although he came to kill him, he called him, "My lord the king!" And he continued, saying:

> "Why do you listen to the words of men who say, 'Indeed David seeks your harm'? Look, this day your eyes have seen that the LORD delivered you today into my hand in the cave, and someone urged me to kill you. But my eye spared you, and I said, 'I will not stretch out my hand against my lord, for he is the LORD's anointed.' Moreover, my father, see! Yes, see the corner of your robe in my hand! For in that I cut off the corner of your robe, and did not kill you."[74]

At that time, Saul wept and said to David, "You are more righteous than I."[75] Do you think that, after this,

---

72   1 Samuel 24:6.

73   1 Samuel 24:8.

74   1 Samuel 24:9–11.

75   1 Samuel 24:17.

Saul stopped chasing David? Not at all! He continued to fight against David, wanting to kill him.

St. Moses the Strong

There are many virtues in the life of St. Moses. One of the most important virtues in his life was the virtue of endurance. It is certain that when St. Moses joined the monastery, many monks kept their distance from him, perhaps because of his background. He was a thief, a gang leader. Therefore, many may not have welcomed him, or at least may have kept their distance from him.

Also, on the day of his ordination as a priest, the Patriarch tried to test him. And as you know, St. Moses was black. So on the day of his ordination, the Patriarch said to him, "What brought you here? Oh you, who is black in color." When the Patriarch kicked him out of the church, St. Moses left the church immediately. He did not get angry, rather he endured the insult. Then the Patriarch brought him back and he ordained him as a priest on that day. And later on, the monks asked him. How did you feel when the Patriarch said that to you and kicked you out of the church. He told them, "I felt like a dog; you tell him, 'Go away,' he goes away. You tell him, 'Come back,' he comes back."

Also, because he was strong in his body, St. Moses used to take the water jugs of the monks by night to go to the water well, which was far away, to fill them up and bring them back, without anybody knowing this. And here we see his endurance.

In the beginning of his monastic life, the demons and the diabolic wars were very harsh on him. And he endured this. On one night, he went to his spiritual father more than ten times. St. Moses was great in the virtue of forbearance and endurance. May we put the example of St. Moses before our eyes. May we learn from him, how to be patient. How to endure and to have a big heart, so that all these hardships and tribulations may not affect us.

3

Why Should I Endure Injustice?

Endurance is a Biblical Commandment

First of all, enduring injustice is a biblical commandment, and we are all called to endure injustice. In his first epistle, St. Peter says, "Servants, be submissive to your masters with all fear, not only to the good and gentle, but also to the harsh,"[76] that is, not only to the kind, nice person, but also the harsh. Then he continues, saying, "For this is commendable, if because of conscience toward God one endures grief, suffering wrongfully."[77] What does "enduring because of conscience toward God" mean? While you can talk back politely to the one speaking with you, or you can answer "eye for eye, and tooth for tooth," or you can ignore them completely and not answer them, or any other kind of reaction, here however he

---

76   1 Peter 2:18.
77   1 Peter 2:19.

is saying to you: "For this is commendable, if because of conscience toward God one endures grief, suffering wrongfully." Then he continues, saying, "For what credit is it if, when you are beaten for your faults, you take it patiently?"[78] That is to say, if I did something wrong, and then someone yelled at me, and I remain silent and endure it, here I deserve it because I had done something wrong. Then he goes on to say, "But when you do good and suffer, if you take it patiently, this is commendable before God,"[79] meaning that, if I am walking uprightly, and then someone rebukes me or yells at me, and I take it patiently, this is commendable before God.

The marvelous thing is that he says, "For to this you were called,"[80] referring to enduring injustice, and he continues, "because Christ also suffered for us, leaving us an example, that you should follow His steps,"[81] that is, the Lord Christ suffered injustice. In the Divine Liturgy according to St. Gregory, taken from Isaiah, he says, "You have borne the oppression of the wicked." For the Lord Christ not only endured so that salvation be accomplished, but He also endured to give us an example, so that we may follow in His footsteps. So, what is the example He left for us? "Who committed no sin, nor was deceit found in His mouth."[82] This

---

78   1 Peter 2:20.

79   Ibid.

80   1 Peter 2:21.

81   Ibid.

82   1 Peter 2:22.

means that any suffering the Lord Christ endured, He was treated unjustly in it. He "who, when He was reviled, did not revile in return; when He suffered, He did not threaten, but committed Himself to Him who judges righteously."[83] St. Paul the Apostle says, "Being reviled, we bless; being persecuted, we endure; being defamed, we entreat."[84] St. Peter also says, "For it is better, if it is the will of God, to suffer for doing good than for doing evil. For Christ also suffered once for sins, the just for the unjust."[85]

Sometimes we ask, "Why is he treating me in this manner? Why this injustice?" This question itself is wrong. It will produce within us some kind of anger and intolerance. Therefore, we, as children of God, must program ourselves to endure injustice because of conscience toward God. You may say that the Holy Scriptures encourage iniquity and make the iniquitous increase in their iniquity. I will say to you, no, because when the Holy Scriptures speak to the one who is treating unjustly, it is different from when they speak to the one who is unjustly treated. The first epistle to the Corinthians speaks about the story of how one person might take his brother to civil courts for judgment, not his brother according to the flesh, but rather his believing brother. St. Paul the Apostle says that civil courts do not judge according to the laws of God; therefore, he is considered to be judged by unjust men.

---

83   1 Peter 2:23.

84   1 Corinthians 4:12–13.

85   1 Peter 3:17–18.

St. Paul the Apostle say, "Now therefore, it is already an utter failure for you that you go to law against one another. Why do you not rather accept wrong? Why do you not rather let yourselves be cheated?"[86] He means to say that it is rather better for you to go to sleep wronged and cheated, than to take your unjust brother to court. Then he says, "No, you yourselves do wrong and cheat, and you do these things to your brethren! Do you not know that the unrighteous will not inherit the kingdom of God?"[87] For the harsh person, who wrongs his brother, especially in closed communities, like monasteries, will not inherit the kingdom of God—that is, the who wrongs his brother, slanders him, pushes him around, or bosses him around.

Endurance of Injustice Equips the Person for Life

I also have weaknesses and need others to be patient with me. And so long as I need others to be patient with me, I must also be patient with others. For the day will come when I will be weak and agitated, and will want others to be patient with me; and so I must be patient with others also. The person, who has gotten used to endurance, if they fall sick—God forbid—they would have already become accustomed to endurance. If they lose someone dear to them, they would have already become accustomed to endurance. If persecution

---

86   1 Corinthians 6:7.

87   1 Corinthians 6:8–9.

comes upon the Church, and Christians begin to be killed, they would have already become accustomed to endurance. Endurance then prepares the person to endure greater things in life in general.

Endurance is the Way of Perfection.

Endurance also is the way of perfection. St. James says, "My brethren, count it all joy when you fall into various trials, knowing that the testing of your faith produces patience. But let patience have its perfect work."[88] That is, he is saying that when you fall into a trial, endure—but endure to the end; and then he says, "That you may be perfect and complete, lacking nothing."[89] This means that when you endure and are patient, this makes you a perfect person: "That you may be perfect and complete, lacking nothing." Endurance is the way of perfection.

---

88   James 1:2–4.

89   James 1:4.

4

How do I endure Injustice?

Now that we understand that we are called to endure, then comes the important question: But how do I endure? How do I attain to positive endurance? How do I endure, without being troubled? We will mention seven points that will explain to us how to endure.

1. You Cannot Endure Without Divine Grace

Concerning how the Lord Jesus Christ prepared Himself for the cross, St. Paul says in Hebrews, "Who, in the days of His flesh, when He had offered up prayers and supplications, with vehement cries and tears to Him who was able to save Him from death, and was heard because of His godly fear."[90] How did the Lord Jesus Christ prepare Himself for the cross, to endure trials, spitting, being struck with their hands on His cheek, mocking—how did He endure all this? Through prayer:

---

90   Hebrews 5:7.

"He had offered up prayers and supplications, with vehement cries and tears." He prayed and wept, to the point that His sweat fell as drops of blood: "He had offered up prayers and supplications, with vehement cries and tears to Him who was able to save Him from death, and was heard because of His godly fear," through the resurrection, because Christ rose up from the dead.

Therefore, when someone treats me harshly, and I am troubled and very distressed, I need to go with Christ to Gethsemane; I need to kneel there and pray and pour out tears before God. And I need to cry out to God and ask Him, saying, "You are able to save me; You are able to give me grace to endure. Lord, grant me the grace of positive endurance, enduring with joy. Lord, You said, 'Ask, and it will be given to you.'" His Holiness Pope Shenouda expressed this in a poem, writing, "Shut the door and dispute in the blackness of the night with Jesus…. Tell Him, 'It has intensified and become difficult, so open the wide door.' Tell Him, 'I am powerless and unable.'" Stand and pray and ask the Lord. Say to Him, "It has intensified and become difficult. Lord, You are the one who will give me endurance and a stout heart that can endure."

2. You Need to Accustom Yourself to Being Patient

H.H. Pope Shenouda used to deal with hard times through three phrases: "Our Lord is present; it is bound to end; it is all for the good." These are taken from verses. "Our Lord is present" is taken from the epistle to the Romans: "If God is for us, who can be against us?"[91] For God is present. "Call upon Me in the day of trouble; I will deliver you, and you shall glorify Me."[92] Isaiah says in the Old Testament, "In all their affliction He was afflicted, and the Angel of His Presence saved them."[93] David always cried out to the Lord in the day of trouble. So do not be afraid; God is present. God is with me in tribulation; God is with me in the furnace of fire; God is with me in the den of lions; God is with me in prison: "If God is for us, who can be against us?"[94] And in Midnight Praises and the Absolution of the Priests, we beseech our Lord to do justice for those unjustly treated [or the oppressed]. For the Lord is always standing with the oppressed. Therefore, if you are on the side of the oppressed, be assured that our Lord is with you, but if you are on the side of the oppressor, if you do not repent, then be assured that our Lord is not with you. This is the first phrase.

The second phrase—"it is bound to end." Either way, it will end; be patient, and it will end. Perhaps you were not contemporaries of the events of 1981, with President Sadat. We could not perceive an end to them, and those who were close to Sadat said that

---

91 Romans 8:31.

92 Psalms 50:15.

93 Isaiah 63:9.

94 Romans 8:31.

he harbored very bad intentions against the Church, the bishops, priests, and laity, who were in prison— and against Pope Shenouda. Nevertheless, our Lord ended it in less than forty days, in less than a month in a way which no one had anticipated or imagined, and which was in no one's consideration. David went through many tribulations at the hand of Saul, but the tribulations ended, and he became a king. Then his son Absalom revolted against him, and it also ended. Therefore, it is bound to end. Every matter will end. So be patient, and it will end.

The third phrase—"it is all for the good." St. Paul the Apostle said in the epistle to the Romans, "All things work together for good to those who love God.[95] He did not say "some things" or "most things," but "all things." Indeed it is all for the good. Train yourself to be patient; learn from Job. He said to his wife, "You speak as one of the foolish women speaks. Shall we indeed accept good from God, and shall we not accept adversity?"[96] I mean, if the Lord takes you to the mountain of Transfiguration, you say, "Lord, it is good for us to be here;"[97] and if He takes you to Gethsemane, the mountain of prayer and praise, you fall asleep with Peter, James, and John, and you become lazy and do not pray; and if He takes you to Golgotha, you run away and deny Him and betray Him. All of us want to be on the mountain of Transfiguration only.

---

95   Romans 8:28.

96   Job 2:10.

97   Matthew 17:4.

This is foolishness, as Job said to his wife, "You speak as one of the foolish women speaks."[98] If our Lord permitted a trial, I should endure it. Job said, "The Lord gave, and the Lord has taken away; Blessed be the name of the Lord."[99] St. Paul the Apostle said, "By evil report and good report."[100] If people praise me, it will pass; if they disparage me, it will also pass. What is the problem? You need patience.

Train yourself to be patient: "By your patience possess your souls."[101] The opposite of "possess" is "lose." Therefore, without patience you will lose yourself. Nowadays we want to receive everything quickly, and we have lost the virtue of endurance and patience, but St. James said, "We count them blessed who endure. You have heard of the perseverance of Job and seen the end intended by the Lord."[102]

3. Love

If I am filled with the Holy Spirit and have the fruit of the Spirit in my life, then I have love. Love "bears all things, … endures all things."[103] For this reason, the Church reminds us of the epistle to the Ephesians in the morning every day, in the Morning Hour of the

---

98   Job 2:10.
99   Job 1:21.
100 2 Corinthians 6:8.
101 Luke 21:19.
102 James 5:11.
103 1 Corinthians 13:7.

Agpeya: "Bearing with one another in love, endeavoring to keep the unity of the Spirit in the bond of peace."[104] When we bear with one another, there will be unity among us. "The love of God has been poured out in our hearts by the Holy Spirit who was given to us."[105] For this reason your spiritual canon is important, attending the Divine Liturgy is important, attending Midnight Praises is important, because these are the means through which the Holy Spirit will fill you. This is the oil; the Holy Spirit is the oil. How will He fill my lamp? Through prayer, Liturgy, Midnight Praises, spiritual books, prostrations, fasts. This is the way through which the Holy Spirit will fill me.

In the first epistle to the Corinthians, we read that love "bears all things, believes all things, hopes all things, endures all things."[106] There is an Arabic saying that says that if someone loves you, he will endure and be patient with you, but your enemy lies in wait for you to make a mistake. This is very true. If I love someone, I will let it go; I will endure. But if I do not love, I will be lying in wait to catch the person in a word he might say. Lack of endurance is lack of love.

That is why, in the First Hour in the Agpeya, we read a passage from the epistle to the Ephesians. And who wrote this passage? St. Paul did, who was a prisoner. I am sure that a person who is a prisoner needs support; he needs somebody to encourage him. But can

104 Ephesians 4:2.
105 Romans 5:5.
106 1 Corinthians 13:7.

you imagine St. Paul, while he was a prisoner, sent the people a message, asking them to endure. He said, "I, therefore, the prisoner of the Lord, beseech you to walk worthy of the calling with which you were called."[107]

God called you. So walk worthy of this calling. How come? What do you expect from me? He continues, saying, "With all lowliness and gentleness, with longsuffering, bearing with one another in love."[108] Bearing with—enduring—one another in love. If we really have the agape love in our life, we will be able to endure one another.

And I want you to reflect on the word "longsuffering." Longsuffering means the ability to suffer for a long time. And longsuffering is one of the fruit of the Holy Spirit. If I am filled with the Holy Spirit, then I will be able to suffer for a long time.

4. Be Understanding Concerning the Weaknesses of Others

There is a verse, which although we all know by heart, yet we do not know how to use it: "Be transformed by the renewing of your mind."[109] The renewing of your mind means that you should think in another way. You can think of the same situation either in a way that agitates you, or in another way that calms you down. The proof of this is that if someone, for example, walks

---

107 Ephesians 4:1.

108 Ephesians 4:2.

109 Romans 12:2.

into a room full of people, and starts to insult them, will all have the same reaction? No, for the reaction will depend upon how the person is thinking. How does the person think about the insult? If someone says, "How dare he yell at us in this way!" then this person will yell back at him. Another might say, "I will receive a crown in heaven. Did not Christ say, 'Blessed are you when they revile and persecute you, and say all kinds of evil against you falsely for My sake. Rejoice and be exceedingly glad, for great is your reward in heaven.'?" Another might say, "This man is crazy. Leave him alone." Your reaction depends on your interpretation of the situation. Therefore, keep your interpretation positive. So long as you keep your interpretation positive, you will endure; but if your interpretation is negative, you will be angry, upset, and agitated. Accustom yourself to have positive interpretation.

This is what I meant by being understanding concerning the weaknesses of others. You may also say, "This may be a weakness he has, and he is struggling against it. I also have many weaknesses, and God is patient with me. I have been confessing the same weakness for the past ten years, and God has been patient with me. Then I will also be patient with him"; If you thought in this way, you would calm down.

If you thought, however, "Why does he treat me in this way? I did him no wrong! Why this injustice? Why this criticism? We are in church—why does he treat me in this way?" then you would be the one heating yourself up. You are setting yourself on fire, and in the end, you will be one who is troubled. It may be that the one who upset you does not care at all. For this reason, you need to be understanding of the weaknesses of others. St. Paul the Apostle says, "We then who are strong ought to bear with the scruples of the weak."[110] That is to say, if you are strong, and there is someone among us who is sick, who is going to support him? Is it someone else who is also weak and sick like him, or another who is strong? Therefore, if you are strong, and you see yourself as such, then you must be patient with others. And if you are weak, and you want others to be patient with you, then you must be patient with others also.

When someone upsets you, look for an excuse for them. On the cross the Lord Jesus Christ said, "Father, forgive them, for they do not know what they do."[111] He made an excuse for them: "For they do not know that I am the incarnate Son of God." He defended them. Therefore, look for excuses for others.

5. Look to the Reward

There is a reward for enduring with the Lord. See what St. Paul said about Christ: "Looking unto Jesus, the author and finisher of our faith, who for the joy that was set before Him endured the cross, despising the shame."[112] What was it that made the Lord Jesus Christ

---

110 Romans 15:1.
111 Luke 23:34.
112 Hebrews 12:2.

endure the cross? Yes, through the cross, the whole world will be saved; through the cross, I will destroy the gates of Hades and bring out those who were in Hades and transfer them to Paradise; through the cross, I will crush death; through the cross, there is victory over the devil and sin. "… for the joy that was set before Him endured the cross, despising the shame, and has sat down at the right hand of the throne of God,"[113] and he continues, saying, "For consider Him who endured such hostility from sinners against Himself."[114] He is saying to you that when you are troubled, feeling that you have been treated unjustly, consider the Lord Jesus Christ who endured from sinners hostility and enmity of such a magnitude against Himself, "lest you become weary and discouraged in your souls."[115]

Consider the reward. In my opinion, St. Stephen said, "Lord, do not charge them with this sin," when he saw heaven and the glory. He said, "These people are not stoning me. With each stone thrown at me, I receive a crown in heaven. Then do not count this as sin against them. This is not a sin, Lord, when someone is giving me all these crowns." At the time of tribulation, what are your eyes focusing on? Are they focusing on heaven and the reward? Or on the tribulation itself? His Holiness Pope Shenouda says that if you place the tribulation between you and our Lord, then you will be upset at the Lord and say,

---

113 Ibid.
114 Hebrews 12:3.
115 Ibid.

"Why did the Lord do this; why did the Lord do that?" Rather, place Christ between you and the tribulation, and then you will have joy and will be comforted. Do not place the tribulation between you and the Lord. Look to the reward.

6. The Intercession of the Saints

You might say, "What is with the intercession of the saints?" For those who deny the intercession of the saints, in the same chapter in Hebrews, St. Paul says, "Therefore we also, since we are surrounded by so great a cloud of witnesses, let us lay aside every weight, and the sin which so easily ensnares us, and let us run with endurance the race that is set before us."[116] What does "so great a cloud of witnesses" mean? How can I run the race with endurance, the race of the spiritual life? With the support of the cloud of witnesses around us. It means that they are supporting us and praying for us. This problem I hand over to St. Mary, that issue to Abba Moses; this matter to St. George, that matter to Abba Anthony. Say to them, "You endured. Teach me how to endure."

7. Hope

Hope is a trust in God, that the Lord will take me out of this problem and will give me the grace of endurance, or He will defend me even after many years. After the

---

116 Hebrews 12:1.

cross, there is resurrection, and after darkness, there is light. Have hope in the Lord even if all doors are closed shut. As we have previously mentioned concerning the events of 1981, with the mind it was hopeless, but the Lord is our hope: "The hope of those who have no hope and the help of those who have no helper."[117] For if you have no help, the Lord is your helper. If you are thinking, "How will these issues be resolved? The person who is causing trouble, how will he change?" Our Lord is the hope: "The hope of those who have no hope and the help of those who have no helper."

When you accustom yourself to enduring, you will have peace and joy, and you will preserve the peace wherever you are, and you will receive a blessing, and you will become a perfect man, and you will be praised by the Lord, and you will walk in the footsteps of the Lord Jesus Christ.

Be kind to one another. Do not take the attitude of King Saul; rather, be like David. St. Paul the Apostle says to the Hebrews, "For you had compassion on me in my chains, and joyfully accepted the plundering of your goods."[118] Who is the person who accepts the plundering of his goods joyfully? He here explains the verse, "Be transformed by the renewing of your mind."[119] How do they change their thought? He continues, saying, "Knowing that you have a better and

---

117 Offering of Morning Incense.

118 Hebrews 10:34.

119 Romans 12:2.

an enduring possession for yourselves in heaven."[120] You plunder my goods on the earth, so what? My treasure is in heaven. It makes no difference with me. I am not upset; I am rather joyful: "Joyfully accepted the plundering of your goods."

St. Paul says, "Looking carefully lest anyone fall short of the grace of God; lest any root of bitterness springing up cause trouble, and by this many become defiled."[121] Do not be this person, who does not have the grace of God. Do not be the person who embitters those around him, causing trouble in the community. Do not be the person by whom others become defiled, through a thought of judging someone, a thought of anger, a thought of revenge, and so on. Do not be this character. The problem is that many such people are blind, not seeing that they are so. Be kind. Be like Philemon, of whom it was said, "For we have great joy and consolation in your love, because the hearts of the saints have been refreshed by you, brother."[122] What a very beautiful saying! He is saying that he was the cause of joy and consolation to all the members of the Church, young and old—"the hearts of the saints have been refreshed by you, brother." Choose to be like the one in the epistle to the Hebrews or like Philemon. This is your choice. When we all become like Philemon, the Church will grow more and more, and we will live in peace and love to one another.

---

120 Hebrews 10:34.
121 Hebrews 12:15.
122 Philemon 1:7.

5

What Helps the Virtue

of Endurance Grow?

1. Love

Love is a very key motive to grow in the virtue of endurance. St. Paul says, "[Love] endures all things."[123] When we love one another, we will endure the weaknesses of one another. St. Paul, whose heart was full of love, said, "Being reviled, we bless; being persecuted, we endure."[124] Also, when we remember how God is long-suffering with us, and how He is patient with us, this will make our heart big enough to endure others. Also, when we acquire the virtue of meekness and gentleness, this will help us endure, for a gentle person, a kind person, a meek person usually has a big heart and can endure others easily.

---

123 1 Corinthians 13:7.

124 1 Corinthians 4:12.

2. Winning Others

Another thing that helps us acquire the virtue of endurance is having a sincere desire to win other people. One of the beautiful sayings in the paradise of the fathers is the word that was given to a novice. They said to him, "Make everyone in the monastery bless you."[125] When you have this sincere desire, to get the blessings of others and to win the love of others, you will endure and be patient with them. As St. John Chrysostom said:

> For this reason Paul did not stop even here in his exhortation, but when he has emptied each side of wrath he proceeds to correct their disposition, saying, "be not overcome of evil." "For if," he says, "you continue to bear resentment and to seek revenge you seem indeed to conquer your enemy, but in reality you are being conquered by evil, that is, by wrath: so that if you wish to conquer, be reconciled, and do not make an attack upon your adversary;" for a brilliant victory is that in which by means of good, that is to say by forbearance, you overcome evil, expelling wrath and resentment.[126]

---

125 See *Bustan Al-Rohban Al-Mowasah, Al-joz' Al-Awal* [The Expanded Paradise of the Monks, Vol. 1]. (Egypt: St. Macarius Monastery, 2006), 44.

126 St. John Chrysostom, *Homily to Those Who Had Not Attended the Assembly* 6. (NPNF[1] 9).

3. Strength

Also, St. Paul said, "We then who are strong ought to bear with the scruples of the weak."[127] So, you can endure when you are filled with the Spirit of God, because the Spirit of God is the Spirit of might, the Spirit of power. As the Holy Scripture tells us, "You did not receive the spirit of timidity, but you receive the spirit of power."[128] The Lord said to the disciples, "Tarry in the city of Jerusalem until you are endued with power from on high."[129] When we are filled with the Spirit, and we have strength in our character, then we will be able to endure.

4. Be a Good Example for Others

Also remember that every time you do not endure, you lose your peace. And you are not patient. You set a bad examples before others, which is exactly the opposite of what the Lord told us, "Let your light so shine before men, that they may see your good works and glorify your Father in heaven."[130] See, after almost 1600 years, we remember the endurance of St. Moses, and his light is shining upon us until today, and we are learning from him.

---

127 Romans 15:1.

128 Cf. 2 Timothy 1:7.

129 Luke 24:49.

130 Matthew 5:16.

5. Seek Excuses for Others

To help you grow in enduring others, you should find excuses for them. And when I say, "find excuses," I am speaking about finding real excuses. Like the Lord on the cross, He said, "Father, forgive them, for they do not know what they do,"[131] which was a real excuse. They did not know that He is the Messiah, the Son of God. When you find excuses for others, this will help you to endure them.

6. Accepting Undeserved Honor

Another point that helps you grow in endurance is that you should think about the many times you received undeserved honor and glory. So if sometimes you receive an insult, or are wrongly treated, or go through a hardship that you do not deserve, as you accepted all this honor and praise that you did not deserve, accept this too.

Our problem is that we forget what we received while we are unworthy. Or we take it for granted as if we deserved all these things. That is why when anything trivial or minor happens to us, we lose our peace and become angry. Remember how many times you received honor and glory that you do not deserve. So if something [negative] happened to you that you also do not deserve, you need to accept it.

These are the same words of job to his wife. When

131 Luke 23:34.

he said to her, "Shall we indeed accept good from God, and shall we not accept adversity?"[132]

Let us pray that the Lord may help us to acquire and to grow this virtue of endurance, because in our life on earth, whether we like it or not, we will face many hardships.

---

132 Job 2:10.

www.ingramcontent.com/pod-product-compliance
Lightning Source LLC
Chambersburg PA
CBHW021223020426
42331CB00003B/445